Once Upon A Galaxy

By
10C

First published by AuthorHouse 09/22/05

ISBN: 1-4208-8172-8 (sc)

Printed in the United States of America
Bloomington, Indiana

This book is printed on acid-free paper.

author HOUSE

1663 LIBERTY DRIVE
BLOOMINGTON, INDIANA 47403
(800) 839-8640
www.authorhouse.com

Instructions:
If you find this book, read it as a bedtime story to all those who wish to hear it. With any luck, it will help to further kindness, understanding, creativity, persistence, patience, and reasoning leading to improved advancement of universal harmony.

The author has traveled since early childhood and can vouch for the fact that all people deserve a safe and supportive environment to fulfill their lifetime potential. Additionally, the writer can assure the reader that violence is a total waste of time, energy, resources, and can only lead to more violence. In a world where our resources are very limited and natural disasters could well occupy the majority of our time, violence is not only a primitive response, but extremely wasteful.

One way to reduce violence is by promoting the use of diplomacy, compassion, and logic. Another way to ensure a balanced future is to support leaders that stride to unify the people of the world and not divide them. One warning signal to watch for is a government that neglects the education of the people in order to make the decisions for them. A government should carry out the will of the people, not have the people carry out the leaders' will.

10C attended 13 different schools in several different countries and found that most kids just want to enjoy life.

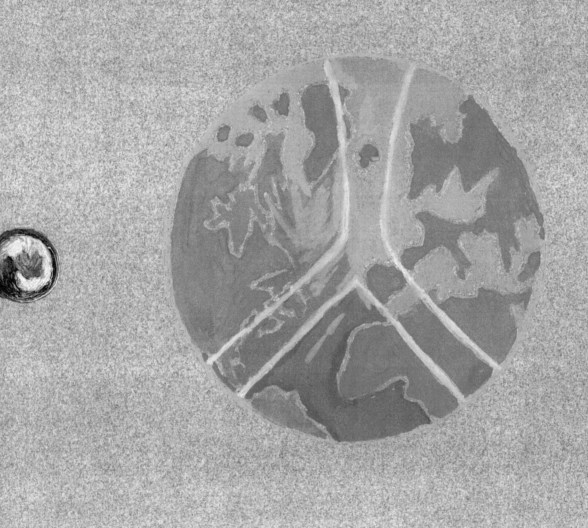

This book is dedicated to all the dreamers,
You know who you are.
All My Love and Prayers,
10C

Once upon a galaxy, there was a planet called Geometrix. On this planet there was a wonderful country called Allshapelandia. In Allshapelandia lived many Shaplings of all kinds, sorts, colors, and sizes.

The Shaplings lived together putting all their unique talents together to make Allshapelandia a wonderful place. They played together, celebrated together, and worked together, and were able to make great progress in helping each other live happy lives. Everyone was special and encouraged to follow their dreams.

In Allshapelandia lived a little Shapling named Spirulina. Spirulina was a little Spiral with a sweetness that made her shine. She liked to get involved in different projects, and enjoyed making new friends.

Not all of Geometrix was as nice as Allshapelandia. Far away on the other side of the planet was another country called Pyrafungula. This land was not as nice. There were only two kinds of Shaplings that lived there, Funnels and Pyramids. They were always fighting each other. They wasted all their time and energy hurting each other. They would not try to get along, and would not stop fighting. They had a very hard life. They were not able to get ahead, since they spent most of their efforts plotting against each other. They had large shortages, because they spent their goods on making weapons to destroy each other instead of on the things they needed.

There was a little Pyramid Shapling named Pyrrie. Pyrrie was sad. His parents had died in the fighting against the Funnels. Pyrrie had a hard life, and depended on odd jobs to get by. He lived in a small corner of a dump. He did not want to fight. He just wanted to be able to enjoy life. One day, he decided to run away from Pyrafungula. He didn't know how he would do it. He had heard that across the large vast empty zone was a country called Allshapelandia, where everyone got along.

Pyrrie decided to ask around about Allshapelandia. Which direction was it in? How far? How long would it take to get there, and how could you get there? He went to the library to see if he could find out answers to his questions, but the books were falling apart and were in such bad condition that he couldn't make any sense of them. He asked many elders, but they had only old memories of stories that were told to them. Some travelers who were passing through the territories had electronic scrolls that showed photographs of parts of Allshapelandia, but they wouldn't allow him to look at them. He could just peek from afar to see screen images from exchanged conversations and news broadcasts.

So one day, he decided to find a new way, to find things out. He wrote a note on the backside of a paper bag. In the note he included a picture of himself, and his location on Geometrix with the degrees of longitude and latitude of his home in the dump, and a request to visit Allshapelandia.

He gave the note to one of the travelers named Zinc, who came through from time to time. Zinc had never gone to Allshapelandia, but he boasted that he would be taking vacation there soon. Pyrrie listened to Zinc talk to the elders and asked him to drop the note at the door of the first home he encountered when he reached Allshapelandia. Zinc was from another region called Metalite. He would sell metal to the Pyrafungulans to make their canons and weaponry. He felt sorry for Pyrrie and promised that he would do him the favor.

As fate would have it, Zinc finally went to vacation in Allshapelandia. Just before going to the resort he had reservations at, he remembered Pyrrie's request and dropped the note at the door of the first home he encountered. It was the home of Spirulina.

Spirulina was on her way to school. She liked to play a triangle in her music class. She opened the note, and was surprised with the picture of Pyrrie in the note. He reminded her of her triangle. She wondered how she would ever be able to help Pyrrie. She stayed after her Music class to show the note to her Music teacher, Mr. Cone, and ask him what she should do.

Mr. Cone suggested that she tell the class about Pyrrie's request to visit. They could give a special concert ball dance and sell tickets to raise funds to pay for Pyrrie's ticket to come and visit. Spirulina was overjoyed! She would start working on this project as soon as possible.

The next Music class, Mr. Cone and Spirulina told the rest of the class about the idea to help Pyrrie come and visit. They all split up all the tasks to get the concert ball dance in swing. Some students made decorations, some the tickets and flyers, others made snacks and festive punch, and others sold the tickets. The class practiced as often as they could, songs that people liked to dance to.

The night of the dance came, and was a great success! Everyone enjoyed the ball. They earned enough to help Pyrrie come and visit. They purchased the ticket to bring Pyrrie to Allshapelandia to visit.

Amazingly, Pyrrie was found by the delivery company with the directions he put on his note. He was taken by the elders to the traveling platform to be picked up and taken on a clipper across the vast empty zone riding on the asteroid belt that ran around Geometrix.

The belt could be unpredictable at times, but it was the best way to get around the planet. Outside the clipper, the belt's mini asteroids seemed like a flash of purple around them.

Pyrrie could hardly believe his eyes when he reached Allshapelandia. Everything was so beautiful, clean, and exciting. The Shapelings were so happy and nice to each other. They were so nice to him. Spirulina, Mr. Cone, and her Music class came to greet him. Sprirulina's parents allowed Pyrrie to stay at their home. That night they had a big party.

The days that followed were a dream come true for Pyrrie. He was able to go to Spirulina's school and read books in the library, play in the playground, eat in the cafeteria, and make so many new friends. Pyrrie did not want to go home. He really wanted to have a chance for a future like Allshapelandia could give him. He finally decided to ask Spirulina's parents what he should do. Spirulina's parents went to the judge and asked how they could help Pyrrie.

The judge said he would try to find Pyrrie a good home in Allshapelandia. Mr. and Mrs. Cone volunteered to give Pyrrie a good home. Pyrrie was adopted by Mr. and Mrs. Cone. They had become very fond of him and came to love him very much.

So it was that Pyrrie was able to stay, and grow to become a great citizen of Allshapelandia. He became a great architect. He was very happy, but there was something he could not forget. He would never forget how lucky he was, and how sad things were for Pyrafungulans.

One day he was walking along and saw a person he recognized, it was Zinc. He called to him, and at first Zinc hardly recognized him. Pyrrie explained to him that he was the Shapling that Zinc had carried the note for. He thanked him and told him all the fine things that had happened to him after Zinc had left his note at Spirulina's house.

He asked Zinc how things were in Pyrafungula. Zinc told him that things were worse than ever. He said that Shaplings there had lost hope. They kept fighting and never stopped. They just had no idea how to change the direction of their lives. Pyrrie was disgusted at first, but after he felt sorry for those he had left behind.

He decided to write a letter to the leaders of Pyrafungula, and tell them of his story, and how futile fighting was. He told them that if they could try to stop fighting long enough to get other things done, they could slowly make Pyrafungula as wonderful as Allshapelandia. He told them it was worth a try. He also told them that he would not return to Pyrafungula until things were different, and would encourage others to leave as well. He sent the letter back with Zinc, who had run out of metal to sell the Shapelings there, so now the Shapelings of Pyrafungula were using fiery gasses instead. Pyrafungula had become a mess.

Sure enough the letter hit a nerve, the leaders were shocked to know of someone who was able to leave and learn to enjoy life. They were jealous. Why shouldn't they have a nice life as well? They had a special meeting to discuss a break from the fighting.

The first week that the Pyrafungulans stopped fighting they could hardly believe the peace and quiet. Soon they started helping each other rebuild their towns. They started to look into better businesses that could help give people things they liked and needed, like food, clothing, homes, and toys.

The weeks passed, and they started having meetings to coordinate the planning of new roads, bridges, hospitals, schools and even libraries. Pyrrie heard the news about the change and decided to go help too. He decided to build some things that would help Pyrafungulans come together in harmony. He designed parks and playgrounds. He designed theatres and music halls. He even designed museums for art. This was his gift to Pyrafungula. Soon Pyrafungula became a wonderful place for all of its Shapelings, Pyramids and Funnels alike.

As for Spirulina, she loved Pyrrie so much; she decided to ask him to marry her. He loved her too, so they married, and lived happily ever after.

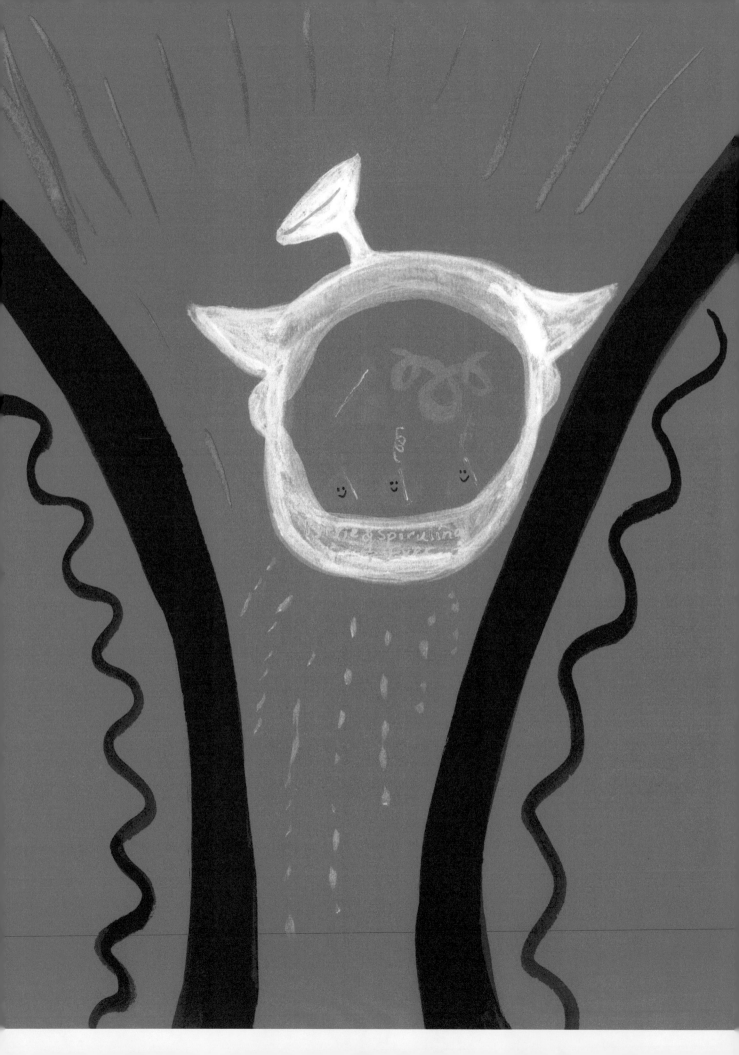

The moral of this story is that bad leaders will divide people and keep them down, but great leaders will bring people together to help them get ahead.

The future is yours. Make the best of it.

About the Author

10C as she is known by friends and family was born in 1959, the oldest child of Amelia Jimenez from Costa Rica and Octavio Allende from Chile.

She graduated from Louisiana State University with a BS in 1983. She married in 1985 and has one son. She earned her Certification as a Clinical Research Associate through the Society of Clinical Research Associates in 1999 and continues a career in managing and monitoring clinical research trials mainly in the oncology therapeutic area in the United States and France.

Prior to college, due to her parents' international careers, she attended 9 different schools and lived in 5 different countries. She realized early on, the impact the environment and the cohesiveness of the society have on the overall wellbeing of children and the vast difficulties that are faced by the majority of them, especially those exposed to violence.

As a young girl, she enjoyed writing and illustrating stories for the other children in her family. Her grandmother, Amparo Rivera Allende, a professional artist, introduced her to drawing and watercolor painting, as a teenager, which she still enjoys to this day.

In 2002, with the assistance of long time friend, and craft master, Donna Bergeron, she designed and sent hundreds of T-shirts to world leaders to encourage more peaceful negotiation towards resolving the Middle East Conflict, and continues to support peace efforts as best she can.

Printed in the USA
CPSIA information can be obtained
at www.ICGtesting.com
LVHW062038111223
766251LV00002B/24